Saving Money Book!

Laurel D. Malvern

Copyright and Legal Disclaimer:

Copyright © 2024 by Laurel D. Malvern

All rights reserved. No part of this book may be reproduced, stored, or transmitted in any form or by any means, electronic, mechanical, photocopying, recording, scanning, or otherwise, without the prior written permission of the publisher, except as permitted by the Copyright Act of 1976.

The information provided in this book, "Saving Money Book," is intended for general informational purposes only. The author, Laurel D. Malvern, is not a licensed financial advisor, accountant, or attorney. The content of this book is based on the author's research, personal experiences, and observations, and it should not be construed as professional financial, legal, or tax advice.

Readers are encouraged to consult with qualified professionals, such as financial advisors, accountants, or attorneys, before making any financial decisions or taking any actions based on the information provided in this book. The author and publisher disclaim any liability for any loss or damage arising from reliance on the information contained herein.

While every effort has been made to ensure the accuracy and completeness of the information presented in this book, neither the author nor the publisher assumes any responsibility for errors, inaccuracies, or omissions. The information provided is subject to change without notice.

References to specific products, services, companies, or organizations within this book are for informational purposes only and do not constitute an endorsement or recommendation by the author or publisher.

By reading this book, the reader acknowledges and agrees to the terms of this copyright and legal disclaimer.

"Saving Money Book"

Chapter Introduction: The Importance of Saving Money in Today's Economy 7

Chapter: Understanding the Challenges of Financial Management 8

Chapter: Setting the Tone for Comprehensive Money Saving 10

Chapter: Understanding Personal Finance: The Foundation of Financial Well-being 13

Chapter: Mastering Financial Literacy: The Key to Financial Empowerment 15

Chapter: Practical Tips for Improving Financial Literacy 17

Chapter: Setting Financial Goals: The Blueprint for Financial Success 20

Chapter: Setting SMART Financial Goals: A Step-by-Step Guide to Success 22

Chapter: Setting Short-Term, Medium-Term, and Long-Term Financial Goals 25

Chapter: Creating a Budget: The Foundation of Financial Stability 28

Chapter: Step-by-Step Guide to Creating a Personalized Budget 31

Chapter: Strategies for Tracking Expenses and Adjusting Your Budget 34

Chapter: Strategies for Saving Money: Practical Tips for Everyday Life 37

Chapter: Strategies for Cutting Expenses, Negotiating Bills, and Finding Alternative Ways to Save 40

Chapter: The Power of Paying Yourself First and Automating Savings 43

Chapter: Building Your Financial Foundation: Tips for Emergency Funds and Major Expenses 46

Chapter: Investing Wisely: Navigating the Fundamentals of Investment 49

Chapter: The Importance of Diversification and Risk Management in Investment Portfolios 52

Chapter: Choosing Investments: Aligning with Risk Tolerance and Financial Goals 55

Chapter: Managing Debt: Mitigating Its Impact on Financial Well-Being 58

Chapter: Efficient Strategies for Paying Off Debt 61

Chapter: The Importance of Avoiding High-Interest Debt and Using Credit Responsibly 64

Chapter: Maximizing Income: Strategies for Increasing Earnings and Financial Security 67

Chapter: Strategies for Negotiating Salary Raises and Promotions 70

Chapter: Maximizing the Value of Existing Income: Tips for Tax Optimization and Benefits Utilization 73

Chapter: Protecting Your Finances: The Importance of Insurance in Financial Planning 77

Chapter: Estate Planning: Guidance on Wills, Trusts, and Preserving Your Legacy 80

Chapter: Safeguarding Against Financial Fraud and Identity Theft 84

Conclusion: Safeguarding Your Financial Future 87

Chapter: Take Action: Transforming Knowledge into Financial Success 90

Chapter: Believe in Your Financial Potential: Achieving Stability and Success Through Saving Money 93

Chapter Introduction: The Importance of Saving Money in Today's Economy

In today's rapidly evolving economy, the importance of saving money cannot be overstated. As we navigate through times of uncertainty, fluctuating markets, and changing financial landscapes, the ability to save money serves as a cornerstone of financial stability and success.

In this chapter, we will delve into why saving money is more crucial than ever in today's economy. We'll explore the myriad of challenges individuals face, from rising living costs to unexpected emergencies, and how saving money can provide a vital safety net in times of need.

As we journey through this chapter, we'll uncover the various benefits of saving money, both in the short term and the long term. From building an emergency fund to achieving financial independence, saving money opens doors to greater opportunities and peace of mind.

Moreover, we'll examine the broader economic implications of saving money on a societal level. By fostering a culture of savings, we not only strengthen individual financial resilience but also contribute to overall economic stability and growth.

So, whether you're just beginning your savings journey or looking to bolster your existing savings habits, join us as we explore the importance of saving money in today's economy and discover the transformative power it holds for your financial future.

Chapter: Understanding the Challenges of Financial Management

In the vast landscape of personal finance, managing one's finances can often feel like navigating a maze fraught with challenges and obstacles. In this chapter, we will explore the common challenges people face when it comes to managing their finances and delve into strategies for overcoming these hurdles.

Lack of Financial Literacy: Many individuals struggle with managing their finances simply because they lack the necessary knowledge and understanding of basic financial concepts. From budgeting to investing, the absence of financial literacy can hinder effective decision-making and lead to costly mistakes.

Debt Burden: The burden of debt is a significant challenge for millions of people worldwide. Whether it's student loans, credit card debt, or mortgages, high levels of debt can weigh heavily on individuals, making it difficult to save money, invest, or achieve financial goals.

Living Beyond Means: In today's consumer-driven society, the temptation to overspend and live beyond one's means is ever-present. Keeping up with the Joneses, impulsive spending habits, and societal pressure to maintain a certain lifestyle can all contribute to financial strain and instability.

Unforeseen Expenses: Life is full of unexpected twists and turns, from medical emergencies to car repairs. Without a robust financial safety net in place, individuals may find themselves ill-equipped to handle these unforeseen expenses, leading to financial stress and hardship.

Procrastination and Lack of Discipline: Procrastination and a lack of discipline are common barriers to effective financial management. Whether it's putting off budgeting, delaying savings contributions, or neglecting to track expenses, procrastination can derail even the best-laid financial plans.

Economic Uncertainty: Economic volatility and uncertainty can pose significant challenges for individuals seeking to manage their finances effectively. Fluctuating interest rates, inflation, job instability, and market fluctuations can all impact financial decisions and strategies.

Despite these challenges, it's important to remember that effective financial management is within reach for everyone. By educating oneself, setting clear financial goals, practicing discipline, and seeking professional guidance when needed, individuals can overcome these obstacles and pave the way toward financial stability and success.

In the following chapters, we will explore practical strategies and actionable advice to help you overcome these challenges and take control of your financial future.

Chapter: Setting the Tone for Comprehensive Money Saving

Welcome to the beginning of your journey towards financial empowerment! In this chapter, we set the tone for our comprehensive approach to saving money – a journey that will equip you with the knowledge, tools, and mindset needed to thrive in today's dynamic economic landscape.

In a world where financial security is increasingly elusive, the importance of saving money cannot be overstated. Whether you're aiming to build wealth, achieve financial independence, or simply gain better control over your finances, the principles of saving money serve as the bedrock upon which all financial success is built.

As we embark on this journey together, it's essential to adopt the right mindset – one characterized by intentionality, discipline, and a long-term perspective. Saving money is not merely about scrimping and sacrificing in the short term; it's about making strategic choices that align with your values and aspirations, while also ensuring financial security and peace of mind for the future.

Our approach to saving money is holistic and multifaceted, encompassing every aspect of personal finance, budgeting, and money management. We understand that saving money is not a one-size-fits-all endeavor; rather, it requires a tailored approach that considers your unique circumstances, goals, and priorities.

Throughout this book, we will explore a diverse array of strategies and techniques for saving money, from budgeting and expense tracking to investing and debt management. Each chapter will build upon the foundation laid here, offering practical insights and actionable advice to help you maximize your savings potential and achieve your financial goals.

But perhaps most importantly, this book is not just about saving money for the sake of saving; it's about empowering you to live a life of abundance, freedom, and fulfillment. By taking control of your finances and making smart choices today, you're laying the groundwork for a brighter and more prosperous future – one where financial worries are a thing of the past.

So, as we dive into the chapters ahead, I encourage you to approach this journey with an open mind and a sense of optimism. By embracing our comprehensive approach to saving money, you're taking the first step towards unlocking a world of financial possibilities. Get ready to transform your relationship with money and embark on the path to financial freedom – it's time to start saving!

Chapter: Understanding Personal Finance: The Foundation of Financial Well-being

Personal finance is the cornerstone of financial well-being, encompassing the management of an individual's financial resources to achieve their financial goals and aspirations. In this chapter, we will define personal finance and explore its significance in shaping our financial futures.

At its core, personal finance is the art and science of managing money effectively. It involves making informed decisions about earning, spending, saving, investing, and protecting one's financial assets. Personal finance is not just about managing day-to-day expenses; it's about creating a comprehensive financial plan that aligns with your values, priorities, and long-term objectives.

The significance of personal finance cannot be overstated. It serves as the foundation upon which all other aspects of financial well-being are built. By mastering the principles of personal finance, individuals can:

Gain greater control over their financial lives: Understanding personal finance empowers individuals to take control of their financial destinies, rather than being at the mercy of economic forces or external circumstances.

Achieve financial goals: Whether it's buying a home, starting a business, or retiring comfortably, personal finance provides the roadmap for achieving your financial aspirations.

Navigate life's financial challenges: From managing debt and unexpected expenses to planning for major life events like marriage and children, personal finance equips individuals with the tools and strategies needed to navigate life's financial ups and downs.

Build wealth and create a legacy: By making smart financial decisions and investing wisely, individuals can build wealth over time and create a lasting legacy for themselves and future generations.

In essence, personal finance is about more than just dollars and cents; it's about achieving financial freedom, security, and peace of mind. It's about living life on your own terms and pursuing your dreams without the constraints of financial stress or uncertainty.

As we delve deeper into the chapters ahead, we will explore the fundamental principles of personal finance and provide practical guidance for mastering this vital aspect of financial well-being. Whether you're a financial novice or a seasoned investor, understanding personal finance is the first step towards unlocking your full financial potential and building the life you desire.

Chapter: Mastering Financial Literacy: The Key to Financial Empowerment

Financial literacy forms the bedrock of sound financial decision-making, enabling individuals to navigate the complexities of personal finance with confidence and competence. In this chapter, we will explore the basics of financial literacy, focusing on essential topics such as budgeting, saving, investing, and debt management.

Budgeting: At its core, budgeting is the process of creating a plan for how you will allocate your income to meet your expenses and achieve your financial goals. A well-crafted budget serves as a roadmap for your financial journey, helping you track your spending, prioritize expenses, and identify areas where you can save money. By mastering the art of budgeting, you can take control of your finances and make informed decisions about how to use your resources effectively.

Saving: Saving money is a fundamental aspect of financial well-being, providing a safety net for emergencies, enabling you to achieve your financial goals, and ultimately helping you build wealth over time. Whether it's setting aside a portion of your income each month, automating your savings, or finding creative ways to cut expenses, cultivating a habit of saving is essential for long-term financial success.

Investing: Investing is the process of putting your money to work in order to generate returns and grow your wealth over time. From stocks and bonds to mutual funds and real estate, there are numerous investment options available to individuals seeking to build wealth and achieve financial independence. By understanding the principles of investing, assessing your risk tolerance, and diversifying your portfolio, you can make informed investment decisions that align with your financial goals and aspirations.

Debt Management: Debt can be a double-edged sword – when used responsibly, it can help you achieve important goals such as purchasing a home or investing in education, but when mismanaged, it can become a significant burden on your financial health. Effective debt management involves understanding your debt obligations, creating a plan for paying off debt, and making strategic decisions about borrowing and repayment. By tackling debt head-on and developing a plan for debt reduction, you can regain control of your finances and move towards a debt-free future.

In conclusion, mastering the basics of financial literacy – including budgeting, saving, investing, and debt management – is essential for achieving financial empowerment and building a solid foundation for long-term financial success. By developing these skills and incorporating them into your financial toolkit, you can take control of your financial destiny and create the life you desire.

Chapter: Practical Tips for Improving Financial Literacy

Improving financial literacy is a journey that begins with a commitment to learning and a willingness to take action. In this chapter, we will explore practical tips and strategies for enhancing your financial literacy and gaining a deeper understanding of personal finance.

Educate Yourself: Take advantage of the wealth of resources available to improve your financial literacy. Read books, articles, and blogs on personal finance, attend workshops and seminars, and explore online courses and educational platforms dedicated to financial literacy. By continuously seeking out new knowledge and perspectives, you can expand your understanding of personal finance and develop the skills needed to make informed financial decisions.

Start Budgeting: Budgeting is the cornerstone of financial literacy, providing a roadmap for managing your income and expenses effectively. Start by tracking your expenses for a month to identify where your money is going. Then, create a budget that allocates your income to essential expenses, savings, and discretionary spending. Regularly review and adjust your budget as needed to stay on track towards your financial goals.

Set Financial Goals: Establishing clear financial goals is essential for guiding your financial decisions and staying motivated on your journey towards financial literacy. Whether your goals include paying off debt, saving for a down payment on a home, or building an emergency fund, setting specific, measurable, achievable, relevant, and time-bound (SMART) goals will help you stay focused and accountable.

Automate Savings and Investments: Take advantage of automation tools and technology to make saving and investing easier and more convenient. Set up automatic transfers from your checking account to your savings or investment accounts each month to ensure consistent contributions. Additionally, consider enrolling in employer-sponsored retirement plans, such as 401(k) or IRA accounts, and take advantage of any employer matching contributions to maximize your savings potential.

Seek Professional Advice: Don't hesitate to seek guidance from financial professionals, such as certified financial planners, investment advisors, or tax professionals, when needed. These experts can provide personalized advice and strategies tailored to your unique financial situation and goals, helping you make informed decisions and optimize your financial outcomes.

Practice Financial Discipline: Cultivate healthy financial habits and exercise discipline in your spending and saving behaviors. Avoid impulse purchases, stick to your budget, and prioritize long-term financial goals over short-term gratification. By developing self-discipline and making intentional choices about how you use your money, you can build a strong financial foundation and achieve greater financial success over time.

In conclusion, improving financial literacy is a lifelong journey that requires dedication, curiosity, and a willingness to learn. By implementing these practical tips and strategies, you can enhance your financial literacy, take control of your finances, and ultimately achieve your financial goals and aspirations.

Chapter: Setting Financial Goals: The Blueprint for Financial Success

Setting clear financial goals is a critical step on the path to financial success. In this chapter, we will explore the importance of setting specific, measurable, achievable, relevant, and time-bound (SMART) financial goals and how doing so can pave the way for a brighter financial future.

Providing Direction and Focus: Setting financial goals provides direction and focus for your financial journey. Whether your goals include buying a home, starting a business, or retiring comfortably, having clear objectives helps you prioritize your efforts and allocate your resources effectively. Without defined goals, it's easy to drift aimlessly and miss out on opportunities for financial growth and prosperity.

Motivating Action: Clear financial goals serve as powerful motivators, inspiring you to take action and make the necessary sacrifices to achieve your objectives. When you have a compelling vision of what you want to accomplish, you're more likely to stay committed to your financial plan and persevere through challenges and setbacks along the way. By anchoring your efforts to specific goals, you can maintain momentum and keep moving forward towards financial success.

Measuring Progress: Setting measurable financial goals allows you to track your progress and monitor your success over time. By breaking down your goals into smaller, actionable steps and establishing key milestones along the way, you can gauge your progress and celebrate your achievements as you move closer to your ultimate objectives. Regularly reviewing your financial goals and assessing your progress enables you to stay accountable and make adjustments as needed to stay on track.

Providing a Sense of Purpose and Fulfillment: Clear financial goals provide a sense of purpose and fulfillment, giving meaning to your financial decisions and actions. When you have an unobstructed vision of what you are working towards and why it matters to you, you are more likely to stay motivated and committed to your financial plan, even when faced with obstacles or temptations to stray off course. By aligning your financial goals with your values and aspirations, you can create a life that reflects your true priorities and brings you greater satisfaction and fulfillment.

In conclusion, setting clear financial goals is a fundamental step towards achieving financial success and building the life you desire. By defining your objectives, staying focused on your priorities, and taking consistent action towards your goals, you can turn your dreams into reality and create a future filled with financial security, freedom, and fulfillment.

Chapter: Setting SMART Financial Goals: A Step-by-Step Guide to Success

Setting SMART (Specific, Measurable, Achievable, Relevant, Time-bound) financial goals is a powerful strategy for achieving clarity, focus, and accountability in your financial journey. In this chapter, we will guide you through the process of setting SMART financial goals, providing a step-by-step framework to help you define objectives that are both meaningful and achievable.

Specific: Begin by defining your financial goals with precision and clarity. Instead of setting vague goals like "save money" or "pay off debt," identify specific outcomes that you want to achieve. For example, your goal might be to save $10,000 for a down payment on a home or pay off $5,000 of credit card debt within the next year. The more specific your goals, the easier it will be to create a plan of action and measure your progress.

Measurable: Make sure your financial goals are quantifiable and measurable, allowing you to track your progress and assess your success over time. Assign specific metrics or criteria to your goals so that you can determine whether you're making progress towards achieving them. For instance, if your goal is to save money, specify the exact amount you want to save and the timeframe in which you aim to achieve it. By quantifying your goals, you can stay accountable and motivated as you work towards your objectives.

Achievable: Set goals that are realistic and attainable given your current financial situation, resources, and capabilities. While it's important to aim high and challenge yourself, setting unrealistic goals can lead to frustration and disappointment. Take stock of your financial resources, income, expenses, and other obligations to ensure that your goals are within reach. Break down larger goals into smaller, manageable tasks to make them more achievable and maintain momentum towards your ultimate objectives.

Relevant: Ensure that your financial goals are aligned with your values, priorities, and long-term aspirations. Ask yourself why each goal is important to you and how achieving it will contribute to your overall financial well-being and happiness. Focus on goals that are meaningful and relevant to your life, rather than pursuing objectives that others may expect or impose on you. By choosing goals that resonate with your values and priorities, you'll be more motivated to stay committed and dedicated to achieving them.

Time-bound: Finally, set deadlines or timeframes for achieving your financial goals to create a sense of urgency and accountability. Establishing specific timelines helps you stay focused and disciplined in your efforts, preventing procrastination, and ensuring that you make steady progress towards your objectives. Break down your goals into smaller, time-bound milestones or checkpoints to keep yourself on track and motivated as you work towards your ultimate targets.

By following these steps and applying the SMART criteria to your financial goals, you can create a roadmap for success and achieve greater clarity, focus, and accountability in your financial journey. Whether you're saving for a major purchase, paying off debt, or investing for the future, setting SMART financial goals will empower you to turn your dreams into reality and build the life you desire.

Chapter: Setting Short-Term, Medium-Term, and Long-Term Financial Goals

When setting financial goals, it's important to consider the timeline over which you aim to achieve them. By breaking down your goals into short-term, medium-term, and long-term objectives, you can create a balanced and comprehensive financial plan that addresses your immediate needs as well as your future aspirations. In this chapter, we will explore examples of each type of financial goal to help you envision your own financial journey.

Short-Term Financial Goals (0-1 years):

Build an emergency fund: Save three to six months' worth of living expenses in a high-yield savings account to cover unexpected expenses or financial emergencies.
Pay off credit card debt: Create a plan to eliminate high-interest credit card debt within the next six to twelve months, prioritizing the highest interest rate balances first.
Save for a vacation: Set aside money each month to fund a short-term vacation or travel experience within the next year, allowing you to enjoy a well-deserved break without going into debt.
Establish a budget: Develop a monthly budget to track your expenses, identify areas where you can cut costs, and free up more money for saving and investing.
Medium-Term Financial Goals (1-5 years):

Save for a down payment on a home: Set a goal to save a specific amount of money for a down payment on a home within the next three to five years, enabling you to achieve homeownership and build equity.

Pay off student loans: Develop a repayment plan to eliminate student loan debt within the next three to five years, freeing up more income for saving, investing, and other financial goals.

Start a business: Launch a small business or entrepreneurial venture within the next two to three years, setting specific milestones and targets for revenue, profitability, and growth.

Save for a major purchase: Whether it's a new car, home renovation, or advanced degree, set a goal to save money for a significant purchase or investment within the next few years, allowing you to achieve your desired outcome without relying on debt.

Long-Term Financial Goals (5+ years):

Retire comfortably: Develop a comprehensive retirement plan to ensure financial security and independence in your golden years, setting a target retirement age and estimating the amount of savings needed to support your desired lifestyle.

Pay off mortgage: Set a goal to pay off your mortgage within the next 15 to 30 years, allowing you to own your home outright and reduce your monthly expenses in retirement.

Build wealth: Accumulate wealth over the long term through strategic investing, saving, and asset allocation, with the goal of achieving financial freedom and leaving a legacy for future generations.

Fund children's education: Save for your children's college education expenses by contributing to tax-advantaged college savings accounts or investment accounts, ensuring that they have access to quality education without taking on excessive student loan debt.

By setting a mix of short-term, medium-term, and long-term financial goals, you can create a balanced and achievable financial plan that addresses your immediate needs while also preparing you for the future. Whether you're focused on building an emergency fund, buying a home, or planning for retirement, having clear goals and a concrete plan of action will help you stay motivated and on track towards financial success.

Chapter: Creating a Budget: The Foundation of Financial Stability

Budgeting is the cornerstone of financial stability and success, providing a roadmap for managing your money effectively and achieving your financial goals. In this chapter, we will explore the concept of budgeting, its role in saving money, and practical strategies for creating a budget that works for you.

What is Budgeting?
Budgeting is the process of creating a plan for how you will allocate your income to meet your expenses, save money, and achieve your financial objectives. It involves tracking your income and expenses, identifying areas where you can cut costs or reallocate resources, and prioritizing spending based on your values and priorities.

Role of Budgeting in Saving Money:
Budgeting plays a crucial role in saving money by helping you:

Track Expenses: By creating a budget, you gain visibility into your spending habits and can identify areas where you may be overspending or wasting money. Tracking your expenses allows you to make informed decisions about where to cut costs and reallocate funds towards savings goals.

Set Saving Goals: Budgeting enables you to set specific savings goals and allocate a portion of your income towards achieving them. Whether you're saving for an emergency fund, a down payment on a home, or retirement, a budget provides a framework for prioritizing saving and staying on track towards your objectives.

Control Spending: A budget helps you exercise discipline and control over your spending by establishing limits and boundaries for different expense categories. By setting spending targets and sticking to them, you can avoid impulse purchases and unnecessary expenses, freeing up more money for saving and investing.

Plan for the Future: Budgeting allows you to plan for future expenses and financial obligations, such as taxes, insurance premiums, and retirement contributions. By incorporating these expenses into your budget, you can ensure that you're adequately prepared and avoid being caught off guard by unexpected costs.

Achieve Financial Freedom: Ultimately, budgeting is a tool for achieving financial freedom and independence. By living within your means, prioritizing saving, and investing, and making strategic financial decisions, you can build wealth over time and create a life that aligns with your values and aspirations.

Practical Strategies for Creating a Budget:

Track Your Income and Expenses: Start by recording all sources of income and tracking your monthly expenses, including fixed expenses (such as rent or mortgage payments) and variable expenses (such as groceries or entertainment).

Identify Your Financial Goals: Determine your short-term, medium-term, and long-term financial goals, and allocate funds towards achieving them within your budget.

Categorize Expenses: Organize your expenses into categories, such as housing, transportation, food, utilities, and discretionary spending, to gain a clear understanding of where your money is going.

Set Spending Limits: Establish spending limits for each expense category based on your income and financial priorities, and adjust as needed to stay within your budget.

Review and Adjust Regularly: Review your budget regularly to track your progress, identify areas where you can cut costs or reallocate funds, and make adjustments as needed to stay on track towards your financial goals.

In conclusion, creating a budget is an essential step towards achieving financial stability, saving money, and ultimately, achieving your financial goals. By adopting a proactive approach to budgeting and incorporating it into your financial routine, you can take control of your finances, reduce financial stress, and build a brighter financial future for yourself and your family.

Chapter: Step-by-Step Guide to Creating a Personalized Budget

Creating a budget tailored to your individual needs and goals is a crucial step towards achieving financial stability and success. In this chapter, we will provide you with a step-by-step guide to creating a personalized budget that aligns with your income, expenses, and financial objectives.

Step 1: Determine Your Income

Start by calculating your total monthly income, including wages, salaries, bonuses, commissions, and any other sources of income.
If your income varies from month to month, use an average based on your recent earnings to create a realistic budget.
Step 2: List Your Expenses

Make a list of all your monthly expenses, categorizing them into fixed and variable expenses.
Fixed expenses are those that remain relatively constant each month, such as rent or mortgage payments, insurance premiums, and loan payments.
Variable expenses are those that can fluctuate from month to month, such as groceries, utilities, transportation, and entertainment.
Step 3: Prioritize Your Financial Goals

Identify your short-term, medium-term, and long-term financial goals, such as building an emergency fund, paying off debt, saving for a down payment on a home, or planning for retirement.

Rank your goals based on their importance and urgency, and allocate funds towards achieving them within your budget.

Step 4: Allocate Funds to Each Expense Category

Determine how much you can afford to spend in each expense category based on your income and financial goals.

Start by allocating funds to your fixed expenses, ensuring that you cover essential costs such as housing, utilities, transportation, and debt payments.

Next, allocate funds to your variable expenses, such as groceries, dining out, entertainment, and discretionary spending.

Finally, allocate funds towards achieving your financial goals, such as saving for emergencies, retirement, or major purchases.

Step 5: Track Your Spending

Keep track of your actual spending throughout the month, comparing it to your budgeted amounts for each expense category.

Use budgeting tools and apps, spreadsheets, or pen and paper to record your expenses and monitor your progress towards your financial goals.

Adjust your budget as needed based on changes in your income, expenses, or financial priorities.

Step 6: Review and Adjust Regularly

Review your budget regularly to assess your progress, identify areas where you can cut costs or reallocate funds, and make adjustments as needed to stay on track towards your financial goals.

Be flexible and willing to adapt your budget as your financial situation changes, taking into account life events, unexpected expenses, and changes in income or expenses.

By following these step-by-step instructions, you can create a personalized budget that reflects your individual needs, priorities, and financial goals. With careful planning and discipline, you can take control of your finances, reduce financial stress, and achieve greater financial stability and success.

Chapter: Strategies for Tracking Expenses and Adjusting Your Budget

Tracking expenses and adjusting your budget as needed are essential practices for maintaining financial health and achieving your financial goals. In this chapter, we will explore effective strategies for tracking expenses and making necessary adjustments to your budget to stay on course towards financial success.

Choose a Tracking Method:

Utilize Budgeting Apps: There are numerous budgeting apps available that make it easy to track expenses, categorize spending, and monitor your budget in real-time. Popular options include Mint, YNAB (You Need a Budget), and PocketGuard.
Spreadsheet: Create a simple spreadsheet using software like Microsoft Excel or Google Sheets to manually track your expenses and budget allocations. Customize the spreadsheet to fit your specific needs and preferences.
Pen and Paper: For those who prefer a more traditional approach, keeping a handwritten journal or notebook to record expenses can be effective. Simply jot down each expense as it occurs and categorize it accordingly.
Categorize Expenses:

Group similar expenses into categories such as housing, transportation, groceries, utilities, dining out, entertainment, and savings.

Be detailed but not overly granular. Aim for a manageable number of categories that provide meaningful insights into your spending habits.

Record Expenses Promptly:

Make it a habit to record expenses promptly as they occur. This ensures accuracy and helps prevent oversights or forgotten transactions.

Use mobile apps or digital tools that allow you to input expenses on the go, making it convenient to track spending in real-time.

Review Regularly:

Set aside time each week or month to review your spending and compare it to your budgeted amounts for each category. Look for patterns or trends in your spending habits, identify areas where you may be overspending or underspending, and assess your progress towards your financial goals.

Adjust Your Budget:

Be flexible and willing to adjust your budget as needed based on changes in your income, expenses, or financial goals.

If you consistently overspend in certain categories, consider reallocating funds from other areas of your budget or finding ways to reduce expenses.

Likewise, if you find that you're consistently underspending in certain categories, consider adjusting your budget to allocate more funds towards your financial goals or discretionary spending.

Plan for Irregular Expenses:

Anticipate and plan for irregular expenses such as annual subscriptions, car repairs, or holiday spending by setting aside a portion of your budget each month in a dedicated sinking fund.

By proactively budgeting for these expenses, you can avoid financial stress and ensure that you're prepared when they arise.

Stay Disciplined:

Stick to your budgeting routine and remain disciplined in your spending habits. Avoid impulse purchases, stick to your budgeted amounts, and prioritize your financial goals. Celebrate your successes and milestones along the way, but also be honest with yourself about areas where you may need to improve or make adjustments.

By implementing these strategies for tracking expenses and adjusting your budget as needed, you can gain greater control over your finances, reduce financial stress, and make steady progress towards your financial goals. Remember that budgeting is a dynamic process that requires ongoing attention and refinement, so stay proactive and stay committed to your financial success.

Chapter: Strategies for Saving Money: Practical Tips for Everyday Life

Saving money is a fundamental aspect of achieving financial stability and reaching your financial goals. In this chapter, we will explore a variety of strategies and practical tips for saving money in your daily life, from cutting expenses to maximizing your savings potential.

Create a Budget:

Start by creating a budget that outlines your income, expenses, and financial goals. Allocate a portion of your income towards saving and set specific savings targets for each month or pay period.
Use budgeting tools or apps to track your spending, identify areas where you can cut costs, and monitor your progress towards your savings goals.
Automate Your Savings:

Set up automatic transfers from your checking account to a dedicated savings account each month. Treat your savings like a recurring expense and prioritize it just like you would any other bill.
Take advantage of employer-sponsored retirement plans, such as 401(k) or IRA accounts, and set up automatic contributions to maximize your long-term savings potential.
Cut Expenses:

Review your monthly expenses and identify areas where you can cut costs or reduce spending. This may include canceling unused subscriptions, negotiating lower bills, or finding cheaper alternatives for everyday expenses.

Look for opportunities to save on recurring expenses such as groceries, utilities, transportation, and entertainment. Use coupons, buy in bulk, carpool, or dine out less frequently to save money over time.

Adopt Frugal Habits:

Embrace frugal living by adopting money-saving habits and practices in your daily life. This may include cooking meals at home, packing your lunch for work, using public transportation, or biking instead of driving, and shopping second-hand or thrift stores.

Avoid impulse purchases and practice mindful spending by asking yourself whether each purchase is truly necessary or aligned with your financial goals before making it.

Prioritize Needs Over Wants:

Differentiate between needs and wants and prioritize spending on essential expenses while cutting back on non-essential or discretionary spending. Focus on meeting your basic needs first, such as housing, food, utilities, and healthcare, before allocating funds towards wants or luxuries.

Delay gratification for non-essential purchases by implementing a "wait-and-see" approach. Give yourself time to consider whether a purchase is truly necessary or whether you can live without it.

Set Savings Goals:

Establish specific savings goals and timelines for achieving them. Whether you're saving for an emergency fund, a vacation, a major purchase, or retirement, having clear objectives will help you stay motivated and focused on your savings efforts.

Break down larger savings goals into smaller, manageable milestones, and celebrate your progress along the way. Consider using visual aids such as a savings thermometer or chart to track your progress and stay motivated.

Maximize Your Income:

Explore opportunities to increase your income through side hustles, freelance work, or passive income streams. Use any additional income to boost your savings or accelerate progress towards your financial goals.

Invest in yourself through education, training, or professional development to increase your earning potential and open up new opportunities for career advancement and financial success.

By implementing these strategies for saving money in your daily life, you can build a strong foundation for financial stability, reduce financial stress, and achieve your long-term financial goals. Remember that saving money is a journey, not a destination, so stay disciplined, stay focused, and stay committed to your financial success.

Chapter: Strategies for Cutting Expenses, Negotiating Bills, and Finding Alternative Ways to Save

In this chapter, we'll explore actionable strategies for reducing expenses, negotiating bills, and discovering alternative methods to save money. These techniques can help you maximize your savings potential and achieve your financial goals faster.

Review Your Monthly Expenses:

Start by examining your monthly expenses in detail. Identify recurring expenses such as rent/mortgage, utilities, groceries, insurance, subscriptions, and discretionary spending.
Look for opportunities to reduce or eliminate unnecessary expenses. Cancel unused subscriptions, downgrade to lower-cost plans, or negotiate better deals on services like cable, internet, or phone.
Negotiate Bills and Contracts:

Don't be afraid to negotiate with service providers to lower your bills. Contact your cable or internet provider and inquire about promotional rates or discounts available to new customers.
For utilities like electricity, gas, or water, explore options to reduce consumption or switch to more cost-effective providers. Some companies offer budget billing plans or energy-saving incentives that can help lower your monthly bills.
Seek Lower Interest Rates:

If you have outstanding debt, such as credit card balances or loans, explore options to lower your interest rates. Contact your creditors and ask about lower interest rates, balance transfer offers, or debt consolidation options.

Consider refinancing high-interest loans, such as student loans or mortgages, to secure a lower interest rate and reduce your monthly payments.

Shop Smarter:

Comparison shop for everyday expenses like groceries, household supplies, and clothing. Look for sales, use coupons, and buy generic brands to save money without sacrificing quality.

Take advantage of cashback and rewards programs offered by credit cards or shopping apps to earn discounts or cashback on your purchases.

Reduce Transportation Costs:

Explore alternative transportation options to reduce commuting costs. Consider carpooling, using public transportation, biking, or walking whenever possible to save on gas, parking, and vehicle maintenance expenses.

If you own a car, practice fuel-efficient driving habits, keep up with regular maintenance, and shop around for the best deals on auto insurance.

Embrace DIY and Frugal Living:

Learn to do-it-yourself (DIY) for tasks like home repairs, gardening, or car maintenance to save money on labor costs. There are countless tutorials and guides available online to help you tackle various projects.

Embrace frugal living by finding creative ways to stretch your dollars. Cook meals at home, pack lunches for work, host potluck dinners instead of dining out, and find free or low-cost entertainment options in your community.

Explore Free and Low-Cost Activities:

Look for free or low-cost activities and entertainment options in your area. Visit local parks, museums, libraries, or community events for inexpensive ways to spend time with family and friends.
Take advantage of free resources like online courses, public libraries, and community centers for personal and professional development without breaking the bank.

By implementing these strategies for cutting expenses, negotiating bills, and finding alternative ways to save, you can significantly reduce your spending and increase your savings over time. Remember that slight changes can add up to significant savings, so stay initiative-taking and keep looking for opportunities to optimize your finances.

Chapter: The Power of Paying Yourself First and Automating Savings

In this chapter, we'll explore the concept of "paying yourself first" and the benefits of automating your savings. These strategies are powerful tools for building wealth, achieving financial goals, and securing your financial future.

Understanding Paying Yourself First:

Paying yourself first is a financial principle that emphasizes prioritizing saving and investing before spending money on other expenses. Rather than saving whatever is left over at the end of the month, you make saving a priority by allocating a portion of your income to savings first.
This approach shifts your mindset from saving what's leftover to saving intentionally, ensuring that you consistently set aside money for your future goals and financial security.
Benefits of Paying Yourself First:

Establishing a Savings Habit: Paying yourself first helps you develop a savings habit by making saving a regular and non-negotiable part of your financial routine.
Building Emergency Funds: By prioritizing saving, you can build emergency funds to cover unexpected expenses or financial setbacks, reducing the need to rely on credit cards or loans.

Achieving Financial Goals: Paying yourself first enables you to make steady progress towards your financial goals, whether it's saving for a down payment on a home, funding your children's education, or planning for retirement.
Reducing Financial Stress: Having savings set aside provides a financial cushion and peace of mind, reducing stress and anxiety related to money management and unexpected expenses.
Automating Your Savings:

Automating your savings involves setting up automatic transfers from your checking account to your savings or investment accounts on a regular basis, such as monthly or bi-weekly.
By automating your savings, you remove the temptation to spend money that should be saved and ensure that you consistently set aside funds for your financial goals.
Many banks and financial institutions offer automatic transfer options, allowing you to schedule recurring transfers and designate specific amounts to be transferred to your savings accounts automatically.
Benefits of Automating Savings:

Consistency: Automating your savings helps you maintain consistency in your saving habits, ensuring that you save regularly without having to think about it.
Discipline: Automation removes the need for willpower and discipline when it comes to saving, making it easier to stick to your savings goals and avoid the temptation to spend impulsively.
Time-saving: Automating your savings streamlines the saving process and saves you time and effort that would otherwise be spent manually transferring money to your savings accounts.

Maximizing Returns: By automating contributions to investment accounts, you can take advantage of dollar-cost averaging and potentially earn higher returns over time through compound interest.

How to Automate Your Savings:

Determine the amount you want to save each month and set up automatic transfers from your checking account to your savings or investment accounts.

Use online banking tools or apps provided by your financial institution to schedule recurring transfers and designate the frequency and amount of each transfer.

Consider automating contributions to retirement accounts such as 401(k) or IRA accounts to ensure consistent retirement savings.

By paying yourself first and automating your savings, you can build wealth systematically, achieve your financial goals, and enjoy greater financial security and peace of mind. These simple yet powerful strategies lay the foundation for a solid financial future and enable you to take control of your financial destiny.

Chapter: Building Your Financial Foundation: Tips for Emergency Funds and Major Expenses

In this chapter, we'll explore practical tips for building an emergency fund and saving for major expenses such as a home or retirement. These financial goals are essential components of a solid financial plan and require careful planning and dedication to achieve.

Building an Emergency Fund:

Start Small: Begin by setting achievable savings goals for your emergency fund. Aim to save at least three to six months' worth of living expenses to cover unexpected costs such as medical emergencies, car repairs, or job loss.

Make it a Priority: Treat your emergency fund as a non-negotiable expense and prioritize saving for it above discretionary spending. Allocate a portion of your income towards your emergency fund each month, even if it means making sacrifices in other areas.

Automate Savings: Set up automatic transfers from your checking account to your emergency fund savings account to ensure consistent contributions. Automating your savings makes it easier to stay disciplined and build your emergency fund over time.

Keep it Accessible: Choose a savings account that offers easy access to your funds, such as a high-yield savings account or money market account. While it's important to earn a competitive interest rate, prioritize liquidity and convenience for emergency purposes.

Saving for a Home:

Determine Your Savings Goal: Calculate how much you need to save for a down payment on a home based on your desired purchase price and the recommended down payment percentage (usually 20% of the home's value).

Set a Timeline: Establish a timeline for achieving your savings goal based on your desired timeframe for purchasing a home. Break down your savings goal into smaller, manageable milestones to track your progress.

Explore Down Payment Assistance Programs: Research down payment assistance programs offered by government agencies, nonprofits, or employers that can help you achieve your savings goal faster. These programs may offer grants, loans, or other incentives to help first-time homebuyers.

Increase Your Income: Look for opportunities to boost your income through side gigs, freelance work, or overtime hours. Consider directing any additional income towards your home savings fund to accelerate your progress.

Saving for Retirement:

Start Early: The earlier you start saving for retirement, the more time your investments have to grow through compound interest. Begin contributing to retirement accounts as soon as possible, even if you can only afford to contribute a small amount initially.

Take Advantage of Employer-Sponsored Plans: If your employer offers a 401(k) or similar retirement plan, take full advantage of it by contributing enough to qualify for any employer matching contributions. Employer matches are essentially free money that can significantly boost your retirement savings.

Maximize Tax-Advantaged Accounts: Contribute to tax-advantaged retirement accounts such as Traditional or Roth IRAs to maximize tax benefits and grow your savings more efficiently. Take advantage of catch-up contributions if you're over 50 to accelerate your retirement savings.

Diversify Your Investments: Invest in a diversified portfolio of stocks, bonds, and other assets to reduce risk and maximize long-term returns. Consider consulting with a financial advisor to develop a personalized investment strategy based on your risk tolerance, timeline, and retirement goals.

By following these tips for building an emergency fund and saving for major expenses like a home or retirement, you can lay the groundwork for a secure financial future and achieve your long-term financial goals. Remember that consistency, discipline, and patience are key to success, so stay focused and committed to your savings goals over time.

Chapter: Investing Wisely: Navigating the Fundamentals of Investment

Investing wisely is a critical aspect of building wealth and achieving long-term financial success. In this chapter, we'll introduce you to the fundamentals of investing, covering various asset classes including stocks, bonds, mutual funds, and real estate. Understanding these investment options will empower you to make informed decisions and build a diversified investment portfolio tailored to your financial goals and risk tolerance.

Stocks:

Stocks represent ownership in a company, giving investors a stake in its assets and earnings. When you buy stocks, you become a shareholder and may benefit from capital appreciation and dividends.
Stocks offer the potential for high returns over the long term but also come with higher volatility and risk. It's essential to research companies thoroughly, assess their financial health and growth prospects before investing in their stock.

Diversification is key to managing risk when investing in individual stocks. Consider building a diversified portfolio of stocks across different industries, sectors, and geographic regions to spread risk and enhance potential returns.

Bonds:

Bonds are debt securities issued by governments, municipalities, or corporations to raise capital. When you buy bonds, you're essentially lending money to the issuer in exchange for periodic interest payments and the return of principal at maturity.

Bonds offer more stability and lower risk compared to stocks but typically provide lower returns. They're considered safer investments, making them suitable for investors seeking income and capital preservation.

Bonds come in various types, including government bonds, municipal bonds, corporate bonds, and treasury bonds. Each type has its risk profile, yield, and tax implications, so it's essential to understand the characteristics of each before investing.

Mutual Funds:

Mutual funds pool money from multiple investors to invest in a diversified portfolio of stocks, bonds, or other assets. They're managed by professional portfolio managers who make investment decisions on behalf of investors.

Mutual funds offer diversification, convenience, and professional management, making them suitable for investors seeking broad exposure to the market with minimal effort.

There are different types of mutual funds, including equity funds, bond funds, index funds, and balanced funds. Each type has its investment objective, risk level, and fee structure, so it's crucial to choose funds that align with your investment goals and risk tolerance.

Real Estate:

Real estate investing involves purchasing, owning, and managing properties for income generation and capital appreciation. Real estate can provide diversification and inflation protection to an investment portfolio.

There are various ways to invest in real estate, including direct ownership of rental properties, real estate investment trusts (REITs), real estate crowdfunding, and real estate partnerships.

Real estate investing offers potential tax benefits, such as depreciation deductions, mortgage interest deductions, and capital gains tax deferral. However, it also requires active management, capital investment, and market expertise.

In conclusion, investing wisely requires a thorough understanding of different asset classes and their associated risks and rewards. By diversifying your investment portfolio across stocks, bonds, mutual funds, and real estate, you can mitigate risk and maximize returns over the long term. Remember to conduct thorough research, seek professional advice if needed, and stay disciplined in your investment strategy to achieve your financial goals.

Chapter: The Importance of Diversification and Risk Management in Investment Portfolios

In this chapter, we'll delve into the significance of diversification and risk management in investment portfolios. These principles are essential for reducing risk, maximizing returns, and achieving long-term financial goals.

Understanding Diversification:

Diversification is the practice of spreading investments across different asset classes, industries, sectors, and geographic regions to reduce risk exposure. The goal is to avoid putting all your eggs in one basket and instead create a portfolio that is less susceptible to the performance of any single investment. By diversifying your portfolio, you can minimize the impact of individual asset volatility and market fluctuations. When one investment performs poorly, others may perform well, helping to offset losses and stabilize overall portfolio returns.

Diversification can be achieved through asset allocation, which involves dividing your investment capital among different asset classes such as stocks, bonds, real estate, and cash equivalents. It can also be achieved within asset classes by investing in a variety of securities or instruments.

Benefits of Diversification:

Risk Reduction: Diversification helps reduce the risk of significant losses by spreading investments across a variety of assets with different risk-return profiles. A well-diversified portfolio is less vulnerable to the adverse impact of market downturns or economic events affecting specific industries or sectors.

Smoother Performance: Diversification can lead to more stable and consistent investment returns over time. While some investments may experience volatility or underperformance, others may provide positive returns, resulting in a smoother overall portfolio performance.

Enhanced Risk-Adjusted Returns: Diversification allows investors to achieve a higher level of return for a given level of risk, known as the risk-adjusted return. By optimizing the risk-return tradeoff, investors can potentially improve portfolio efficiency and achieve their financial objectives more effectively.

Risk Management Strategies:

Asset Allocation: Determine an appropriate asset allocation strategy based on your investment goals, risk tolerance, and time horizon. Allocate your investment capital across different asset classes in proportions that reflect your risk-return preferences and financial objectives.

Rebalancing: Regularly review and rebalance your investment portfolio to maintain your desired asset allocation. Rebalancing involves selling assets that have appreciated in value and reinvesting the proceeds into underperforming assets to restore the original asset allocation.

Portfolio Monitoring: Monitor your investment portfolio regularly to assess performance, identify changes in market conditions, and rebalance as needed. Stay informed about economic indicators, geopolitical events, and industry trends that may affect your investments.

Risk Assessment: Assess and quantify the risk exposure of your investment portfolio using metrics such as standard deviation, beta, and Sharpe ratio. Understand the relationship between risk and return and ensure that your portfolio aligns with your risk tolerance and investment objectives.

In conclusion, diversification and risk management are fundamental principles of sound investment strategy. By diversifying your portfolio across different asset classes and employing risk management techniques, you can reduce risk, enhance returns, and increase the likelihood of achieving your long-term financial goals. Remember to maintain a disciplined approach to portfolio management, stay diversified, and periodically review and adjust your investment strategy as needed to adapt to changing market conditions and financial circumstances.

Chapter: Choosing Investments: Aligning with Risk Tolerance and Financial Goals

In this chapter, we'll provide guidance on selecting investments that align with your individual risk tolerance and financial goals. Understanding your risk tolerance and establishing clear financial objectives are crucial steps in building an investment portfolio that meets your needs and preferences.

Assessing Risk Tolerance:

Risk tolerance refers to your willingness and ability to endure fluctuations in the value of your investments. It's influenced by factors such as your investment horizon, financial situation, investment knowledge, and emotional temperament.

Assess your risk tolerance by considering how you would react to market volatility, investment losses, and fluctuations in portfolio value. Are you comfortable with short-term fluctuations for the potential of higher returns, or do you prefer stability and predictability?

Use risk tolerance questionnaires or assessments provided by financial advisors or online investment platforms to gauge your risk tolerance objectively. These tools typically ask questions about your investment experience, time horizon, investment goals, and willingness to take risks.

Defining Financial Goals:

Clearly define your financial goals, both short-term and long-term, to provide a roadmap for your investment decisions. Common financial goals include retirement savings, education funding, buying a home, starting a business, or building wealth for financial independence.
Determine the timeframe for each goal (short-term, medium-term, or long-term) and the required rate of return to achieve it. Consider factors such as inflation, expected expenses, and any specific milestones or deadlines associated with each goal. Prioritize your financial goals based on their importance and urgency, focusing on those that are most critical to your financial well-being and quality of life.
Matching Investments to Risk Tolerance and Goals:

Conservative Investors: If you have a low risk tolerance and prioritize capital preservation over growth, consider investing in low-risk assets such as bonds, money market funds, and certificates of deposit (CDs). These investments offer stability and income but typically provide lower returns compared to riskier assets.
Moderate Investors: If you have a moderate risk tolerance and seek a balance between growth and stability, consider a diversified portfolio consisting of a mix of stocks, bonds, and cash equivalents. Balanced funds, target-date funds, and diversified mutual funds are suitable options for moderate investors.
Aggressive Investors: If you have a high risk tolerance and are willing to accept greater volatility for the potential of higher returns, consider investing primarily in growth-oriented assets such as stocks, equity funds, and real estate investment trusts (REITs). These investments offer greater growth potential but also come with higher risk and volatility.
Diversification and Asset Allocation:

Regardless of your risk tolerance, diversification and asset allocation are essential principles of sound investing. Spread your investments across different asset classes, industries, sectors, and geographic regions to reduce risk and maximize returns.

Adjust your asset allocation over time based on changes in your risk tolerance, financial goals, and market conditions. As you approach important milestones or your investment horizon shortens, consider shifting towards a more conservative asset allocation to protect your gains and minimize downside risk.

Regular Review and Adjustment:

Regularly review your investment portfolio to ensure that it remains aligned with your risk tolerance and financial goals. Monitor performance, assess risk exposure, and rebalance your portfolio as needed to maintain your desired asset allocation.

Stay informed about changes in the investment landscape, economic conditions, and market trends that may affect your investments. Seek professional advice if needed to make informed decisions and navigate complex investment environments.

By choosing investments that match your risk tolerance and financial goals, you can build a well-balanced investment portfolio that meets your needs and preferences. Remember to stay disciplined, stay diversified, and periodically review and adjust your investment strategy as needed to adapt to changing circumstances and market conditions.

Chapter: Managing Debt: Mitigating Its Impact on Financial Well-Being

Debt can be a significant obstacle to achieving financial well-being and stability. In this chapter, we'll address the issue of debt and explore strategies for managing it effectively to minimize its impact on your financial health.

Understanding Debt:

Debt is money borrowed from creditors or lenders with the obligation to repay it over time, usually with interest. Common types of debt include credit card debt, student loans, mortgages, auto loans, personal loans, and medical bills. While debt can be a useful tool for financing large purchases or investments, excessive debt can lead to financial stress, high interest costs, and limited financial flexibility.
The Impact of Debt on Financial Well-Being:

Debt can have several negative consequences on financial well-being, including:
Financial Stress: High levels of debt can cause anxiety, stress, and sleepless nights as individuals worry about meeting monthly payments and managing debt obligations.
Reduced Disposable Income: Debt repayment obligations can consume a significant portion of your income, leaving you with less money for essential expenses, savings, and discretionary spending.

High Interest Costs: Accumulating interest on debt can result in substantial interest costs over time, making it more challenging to repay debt and achieve other financial goals.
Limited Opportunities: Excessive debt can limit your ability to pursue opportunities such as buying a home, starting a business, or saving for retirement, as lenders may be reluctant to extend credit to individuals with high levels of debt.
Strategies for Managing Debt:

Create a Budget: Develop a budget that outlines your income, expenses, and debt obligations. Allocate a portion of your income towards debt repayment while prioritizing essential expenses and savings goals.
Prioritize Debt Repayment: Focus on paying off high-interest debt first, such as credit card debt, to minimize interest costs and accelerate debt repayment. Consider using strategies such as the debt snowball or debt avalanche method to prioritize and tackle debts systematically.
Negotiate with Creditors: If you're struggling to meet your debt obligations, reach out to your creditors to discuss potential options for repayment, such as negotiating lower interest rates, restructuring payment plans, or seeking hardship assistance programs.
Avoid Taking on New Debt: Resist the temptation to take on new debt unless absolutely necessary. Avoid using credit cards for unnecessary purchases and be mindful of your spending habits to prevent further accumulation of debt.
Build an Emergency Fund: Establish an emergency fund to cover unexpected expenses and financial emergencies, reducing the need to rely on credit cards or loans in times of need.

Seek Professional Help if Needed: If you're overwhelmed by debt or struggling to manage your finances, consider seeking assistance from a certified credit counselor, financial advisor, or debt management agency. These professionals can provide guidance, support, and resources to help you regain control of your finances and overcome debt challenges.

The Path to Debt Freedom:

Achieving debt freedom requires commitment, discipline, and perseverance. By adopting a proactive approach to debt management, developing healthy financial habits, and prioritizing debt repayment, you can gradually eliminate debt and improve your financial well-being.

Celebrate small victories along the way, such as paying off a credit card or reaching a debt milestone. Stay focused on your long-term financial goals and remind yourself of the benefits of becoming debt-free, such as increased financial security, peace of mind, and the ability to pursue your dreams and aspirations.

In conclusion, managing debt effectively is essential for achieving financial well-being and building a solid financial foundation. By understanding the impact of debt, developing strategies for debt management, and committing to debt repayment, you can regain control of your finances, reduce financial stress, and work towards a brighter financial future. Remember that overcoming debt challenges takes time and effort, but the rewards of financial freedom are well worth the journey.

Chapter: Efficient Strategies for Paying Off Debt

In this chapter, we'll explore two popular and effective strategies for paying off debt efficiently: the debt snowball and debt avalanche methods. These methods offer structured approaches to debt repayment, helping individuals prioritize debts, minimize interest costs, and accelerate their journey to debt freedom.

The Debt Snowball Method:

The debt snowball method focuses on paying off debts in order of smallest to largest balance, regardless of interest rate. Here's how it works:

List all your debts in ascending order based on the outstanding balance, from smallest to largest.
Allocate a fixed amount of money each month towards debt repayment, in addition to minimum payments on all debts.
Focus on paying off the smallest debt first while making minimum payments on all other debts.
Once the smallest debt is paid off, roll over the amount you were paying towards it to the next smallest debt.

Continue this process until all debts are paid off.
Benefits of the Debt Snowball Method:

Psychological Momentum: Paying off smaller debts quickly provides a sense of achievement and motivation, creating momentum to tackle larger debts.

Simplified Approach: By focusing on one debt at a time, the debt snowball method simplifies the debt repayment process and helps individuals stay organized and motivated.

Quick Wins: The method prioritizes quick wins, allowing individuals to see progress early on and stay motivated throughout the debt repayment journey.

The Debt Avalanche Method:

The debt avalanche method focuses on paying off debts in order of highest to lowest interest rate, regardless of balance. Here's how it works:

List all your debts in descending order based on the interest rate, from highest to lowest.

Allocate a fixed amount of money each month towards debt repayment, in addition to minimum payments on all debts.

Focus on paying off the debt with the highest interest rate first while making minimum payments on all other debts.

Once the debt with the highest interest rate is paid off, roll over the amount you were paying towards it to the next debt with the highest interest rate.

Continue this process until all debts are paid off.

Benefits of the Debt Avalanche Method:

Interest Savings: By prioritizing debts with the highest interest rates, the debt avalanche method minimizes the total interest paid over time, saving money on interest costs.

Financial Efficiency: The method optimizes debt repayment by focusing on debts that accrue the most interest, helping individuals pay off debt faster and more efficiently.

Long-Term Savings: While it may take longer to see progress compared to the debt snowball method, the debt avalanche method can result in significant interest savings over the long term.

Choosing the Right Method:

Both the debt snowball and debt avalanche methods are effective approaches to debt repayment, but the best method for you depends on your individual preferences, financial situation, and psychological factors.

If you prioritize quick wins and psychological motivation, the debt snowball method may be more suitable for you.

However, if you're focused on minimizing interest costs and achieving long-term savings, the debt avalanche method may be a better fit.

Consider factors such as your debt balances, interest rates, and personal motivations when choosing the right method for paying off debt efficiently.

Additional Strategies for Debt Repayment:

Increase Income: Look for ways to boost your income through side gigs, freelance work, or overtime hours. Use any additional income to accelerate debt repayment and achieve your financial goals faster.

Cut Expenses: Review your budget and identify areas where you can cut expenses or reduce spending. Redirect the money saved towards debt repayment to expedite the process.

Seek Professional Help: If you're struggling to manage your debt or develop a repayment plan, consider seeking assistance from a certified credit counselor or financial advisor. These professionals can provide guidance, support, and resources to help you achieve your debt repayment goals.

In conclusion, paying off debt efficiently requires a structured approach and disciplined commitment. Whether you choose the debt snowball or debt avalanche method, the key is to stay focused, motivated, and consistent in your debt repayment efforts. By implementing these strategies and prioritizing debt repayment, you can accelerate your journey to debt freedom and achieve long-term financial success.

Chapter: The Importance of Avoiding High-Interest Debt and Using Credit Responsibly

In this chapter, we'll delve into the significance of avoiding high-interest debt and utilizing credit responsibly to safeguard your financial well-being and achieve long-term financial success.

Understanding High-Interest Debt:

High-interest debt refers to debt obligations with exorbitant interest rates, typically associated with credit cards, payday loans, and other forms of unsecured borrowing.
These debts often carry double-digit interest rates, compounding quickly and leading to substantial interest costs over time. High-interest debt can become a significant financial burden, making it challenging to repay and hindering your ability to achieve financial goals.
The Impact of High-Interest Debt:

Financial Strain: High-interest debt can place a strain on your finances, consuming a significant portion of your income in interest payments. This can limit your ability to cover essential expenses, save for the future, and achieve your financial goals.
Debt Cycle: High-interest debt can trap individuals in a cycle of debt, where they struggle to make minimum payments and end up accruing additional interest and fees. This cycle perpetuates the debt burden, making it difficult to break free and achieve debt freedom.
Credit Score Impact: Accumulating high-interest debt can negatively impact your credit score, making it harder to qualify for favorable loan terms, secure housing, or obtain employment. A low credit score can limit your financial opportunities and cost you thousands of dollars in higher interest rates over time.
Strategies for Avoiding High-Interest Debt:

Budgeting: Create a budget to track your income and expenses, allowing you to identify areas where you can cut costs and allocate funds towards debt repayment and savings goals.
Emergency Fund: Build an emergency fund to cover unexpected expenses and financial emergencies, reducing the need to rely on high-interest credit cards or loans in times of need.
Lifestyle Adjustments: Adjust your lifestyle and spending habits to live within your means and avoid unnecessary debt. Prioritize needs over wants, and be mindful of impulse purchases that can lead to unnecessary debt accumulation.
Debt Repayment Plan: Develop a structured debt repayment plan to prioritize high-interest debts and pay them off as quickly as possible. Consider using debt repayment strategies such as the debt snowball or debt avalanche method to accelerate debt payoff and minimize interest costs.

Credit Monitoring: Regularly monitor your credit report and credit score to detect any errors or fraudulent activity. Stay vigilant against identity theft and fraud, and take proactive steps to protect your personal and financial information.
Using Credit Responsibly:

Establishing Credit History: Use credit responsibly to establish a positive credit history, demonstrating your ability to manage debt and repay creditors on time. A strong credit history is essential for obtaining favorable loan terms, securing housing, and accessing financial opportunities.
Borrowing Wisely: Borrow only what you can afford to repay and avoid overextending yourself with excessive debt. Be cautious of high-interest credit card offers and predatory lending practices that can lead to financial hardship and debt distress.
Paying Bills on Time: Pay your bills on time each month to avoid late fees, penalties, and negative marks on your credit report. Set up automatic payments or reminders to ensure timely payment of bills and debt obligations.
Monitoring Credit Utilization: Keep your credit utilization ratio low by using only a small percentage of your available credit limit. High credit utilization can negatively impact your credit score and indicate financial distress to lenders.

In conclusion, avoiding high-interest debt and using credit responsibly are essential components of sound financial management. By prioritizing financial responsibility, living within your means, and adopting prudent borrowing habits, you can protect your financial well-being, build a strong credit profile, and achieve your long-term financial goals. Remember that responsible credit use is a key ingredient in achieving financial freedom and security, so approach credit wisely and use it as a tool to enhance your financial future.

Chapter: Maximizing Income: Strategies for Increasing Earnings and Financial Security

In this chapter, we'll explore various ways to maximize income by leveraging side hustles, freelancing opportunities, or advancing in one's career. Increasing income is a crucial aspect of improving financial stability, achieving financial goals, and building long-term wealth.

Side Hustles and Gig Economy:

Side hustles refer to part-time or freelance work undertaken in addition to a primary job or source of income. These side gigs can provide additional income streams and flexibility, allowing individuals to pursue their passions, develop new skills, and boost earnings.

Explore opportunities in the gig economy, such as driving for ride-sharing services, delivering food, pet sitting, tutoring, or offering freelance services in areas like graphic design, writing, or web development.

Choose side hustles that align with your skills, interests, and schedule to maximize earning potential and enjoyment. Consider leveraging online platforms and marketplaces to connect with clients and customers and advertise your services.

Freelancing and Contract Work:

Freelancing involves working as an independent contractor or consultant, offering specialized services or expertise to clients on a project-by-project basis. Freelancers have the flexibility to set their rates, choose their projects, and work remotely, providing opportunities for increased income and autonomy.

Identify your unique skills, talents, and expertise that you can offer as a freelancer. Develop a portfolio showcasing your work and expertise to attract clients and establish credibility in your field.

Leverage online freelancing platforms such as Upwork, Freelancer, or Fiverr to find freelance opportunities and connect with clients worldwide. Network with professionals in your industry and join relevant online communities to expand your freelance network and access potential clients.

Advancing in Your Career:

Advancing in your career is another effective way to maximize income and increase earning potential over time. Invest in your professional development, acquire new skills, and seek opportunities for advancement within your current organization or industry.

Set clear career goals and develop a plan to achieve them, whether it's pursuing further education, obtaining certifications, or seeking promotions or leadership roles.

Build a strong professional network by networking with colleagues, attending industry events, and participating in professional organizations. Networking can provide access to job opportunities, mentorship, and career advancement resources.

Negotiating Salary and Benefits:

Negotiating your salary and benefits is a crucial step in maximizing income and ensuring fair compensation for your work. Research industry standards and salary benchmarks to understand your market value and leverage during negotiations.

Prepare for salary negotiations by highlighting your achievements, skills, and contributions to the organization. Practice negotiation techniques and be prepared to advocate for your worth confidently.

Consider negotiating additional benefits such as flexible work arrangements, professional development opportunities, or performance bonuses to enhance your overall compensation package.

Passive Income Streams:

Passive income streams provide opportunities to earn money with minimal ongoing effort or active involvement. Examples include rental income from real estate investments, dividends from stocks or mutual funds, royalties from intellectual property, or affiliate marketing income.

Explore passive income opportunities that align with your interests, resources, and investment goals. Research and due diligence are essential to identify viable passive income streams and mitigate associated risks.

In conclusion, maximizing income requires a proactive approach, strategic planning, and a willingness to explore diverse opportunities for earning money. By leveraging side hustles, freelancing, advancing in your career, negotiating salary and benefits, and exploring passive income streams, you can increase your earning potential, achieve financial security, and work towards your long-term financial goals. Remember to prioritize your personal and professional development, pursue opportunities aligned with your skills and interests, and remain adaptable and open to new income-generating possibilities.

Chapter: Strategies for Negotiating Salary Raises and Promotions

Negotiating salary raises and promotions is a critical skill for advancing in your career and increasing your earning potential. In this chapter, we'll explore effective strategies for preparing, conducting, and succeeding in salary negotiations to secure the compensation and recognition you deserve.

Preparation is Key:

Research: Begin by researching industry standards, salary benchmarks, and compensation packages for similar roles in your industry and geographic location. Use online resources, salary surveys, and networking to gather relevant data and insights.

Self-Assessment: Reflect on your accomplishments, skills, and contributions to the organization. Identify specific examples of your successes, projects you've led, and results you've achieved to demonstrate your value to the company.

Know Your Worth: Determine your desired salary range based on your research and self-assessment. Be prepared to justify your salary request with evidence of your performance, market value, and the impact you've made on the organization.

Timing and Approach:

Choose the Right Time: Timing is crucial when negotiating a salary raise or promotion. Schedule the conversation at a time when your performance is top of mind for your manager, such as during performance reviews, after completing a significant project, or when the company is in a strong financial position.

Initiate the Conversation: Take the initiative to request a meeting with your manager to discuss your career development and compensation. Frame the conversation positively, emphasizing your commitment to the organization's success and your desire to grow professionally.

Be Confident and Assertive: Approach the negotiation with confidence and assertiveness, but remain professional and respectful. Clearly articulate your value proposition and the reasons why you deserve a salary raise or promotion based on your performance, skills, and contributions.

Presenting Your Case:

Highlight Your Achievements: Showcase your accomplishments, skills, and contributions during the negotiation. Provide specific examples of projects you've successfully completed, goals you've exceeded, and positive outcomes you've achieved for the organization.

Quantify Your Impact: Use metrics, data, and tangible results to quantify your contributions and demonstrate your value to the company. Highlight any revenue generated, costs saved, efficiencies improved, or other measurable outcomes attributable to your efforts.

Emphasize Your Future Potential: Articulate your vision for future growth and development within the organization. Discuss your career goals, aspirations, and how a salary raise or promotion will enable you to contribute even more effectively to the company's success.

Negotiation Techniques:

Aim High, but Be Realistic: Start the negotiation with a salary range that is slightly higher than your desired salary, but within the realm of reason based on your research and market value. Be prepared to justify your salary request with evidence and rationale.

Focus on Total Compensation: Consider negotiating other aspects of your compensation package, such as additional benefits, perks, flexible work arrangements, or professional development opportunities, if a salary raise is not immediately feasible.

Listen and Respond: Actively listen to your manager's feedback and concerns during the negotiation. Be prepared to address any objections or questions raised and adjust your approach accordingly.

Follow-Up and Acceptance:

Document the Agreement: After reaching a mutual agreement on salary raises or promotions, document the details of the agreement in writing, including the new salary, effective date, and any other terms or conditions discussed.

Express Gratitude: Thank your manager for the opportunity to discuss your career advancement and compensation. Express appreciation for their support and commitment to your professional growth.

Continue to Excel: Once the negotiation is concluded, continue to excel in your role and deliver outstanding results to justify your salary raise or promotion. Maintain open communication with your manager and seek feedback on your performance and progress.

In conclusion, negotiating salary raises and promotions requires preparation, confidence, and effective communication skills. By researching industry standards, presenting a compelling case for your value, and engaging in constructive dialogue with your manager, you can increase your chances of success and secure the compensation and recognition you deserve. Remember to approach negotiations with professionalism, positivity, and a collaborative mindset, and strive for win-win outcomes that benefit both you and the organization.

Chapter: Maximizing the Value of Existing Income: Tips for Tax Optimization and Benefits Utilization

In this chapter, we'll explore strategies for maximizing the value of your existing income through tax optimization and utilization of benefits. By taking advantage of tax-saving opportunities and maximizing the benefits offered by your employer or government programs, you can optimize your financial situation and retain more of your hard-earned money.

Understanding Tax Optimization:

Tax optimization involves legally minimizing your tax liability by taking advantage of available deductions, credits, and tax-efficient investment strategies. By optimizing your taxes, you can reduce the amount of taxes you owe and keep more of your income for yourself.

Maximizing Tax-Advantaged Accounts:

Contribute to Retirement Accounts: Take advantage of tax-advantaged retirement accounts such as 401(k)s, IRAs, or Roth IRAs to save for retirement while reducing your taxable income. Contributions to these accounts are made with pre-tax or after-tax dollars, allowing you to defer taxes on investment gains until retirement.

Utilize Health Savings Accounts (HSAs): If eligible, contribute to an HSA to save for qualified medical expenses while reducing your taxable income. Contributions to an HSA are tax-deductible, and withdrawals for qualified medical expenses are tax-free, making HSAs a powerful tax-advantaged savings vehicle.

Claiming Tax Deductions and Credits:

Itemize Deductions: Consider itemizing deductions if they exceed the standard deduction amount, as this can result in lower taxable income and reduce your overall tax liability. Common deductible expenses include mortgage interest, property taxes, charitable contributions, and unreimbursed medical expenses.

Take Advantage of Tax Credits: Explore available tax credits such as the Earned Income Tax Credit (EITC), Child Tax Credit, or Education Credits to reduce your tax bill dollar-for-dollar. Tax credits are more valuable than deductions as they directly reduce the amount of taxes owed.

Utilizing Employer Benefits:

Maximize Retirement Contributions: Take full advantage of employer-sponsored retirement plans such as 401(k)s or 403(b)s by contributing enough to qualify for employer matching contributions. Employer matches are essentially free money and can significantly boost your retirement savings.

Utilize Flexible Spending Accounts (FSAs): If offered by your employer, contribute to a Health Care FSA or Dependent Care FSA to pay for eligible medical or childcare expenses with pre-tax dollars. FSAs can lower your taxable income and save you money on out-of-pocket expenses.

Explore Other Employee Benefits: Take the time to understand and maximize all the benefits offered by your employer, such as health insurance, life insurance, disability coverage, wellness programs, or commuter benefits. These benefits can provide financial protection and savings opportunities that enhance the value of your compensation package.

Managing Investment Taxes:

Invest Tax-Efficiently: Consider investing in tax-efficient investment vehicles such as index funds, exchange-traded funds (ETFs), or municipal bonds to minimize taxable investment income. These investments generate lower levels of taxable distributions or offer tax-free income, helping to reduce your tax burden.

Tax-Loss Harvesting: Implement tax-loss harvesting strategies to offset capital gains and reduce your tax liability. Tax-loss harvesting involves selling investments at a loss to realize capital losses, which can be used to offset capital gains or reduce taxable income by up to $3,000 per year.

Staying Informed and Seeking Professional Advice:

Stay Updated on Tax Law Changes: Keep abreast of changes to tax laws, deductions, and credits that may affect your tax situation. Consult reliable sources of information or seek guidance from tax professionals to ensure you're taking advantage of all available tax-saving opportunities.

Consult a Tax Professional: If you have complex financial situations or questions about tax optimization strategies, consider consulting a tax professional or financial advisor. A tax professional can provide personalized advice and help you navigate the complexities of the tax code to optimize your tax situation effectively.

In conclusion, maximizing the value of your existing income through tax optimization and benefits utilization requires proactive planning, awareness of available opportunities, and strategic decision-making. By taking advantage of tax-advantaged accounts, claiming deductions and credits, maximizing employer benefits, managing investment taxes, and staying informed about tax law changes, you can optimize your financial situation and retain more of your income for your present and future financial needs. Remember that tax optimization is an ongoing process, so review your strategies regularly and adjust them as needed to adapt to changes in your financial situation and the tax landscape.

Chapter: Protecting Your Finances: The Importance of Insurance in Financial Planning

In this chapter, we'll explore the critical role of insurance in financial planning and how various types of insurance, including health, life, and property insurance, can safeguard your financial well-being and provide peace of mind in times of uncertainty.

Understanding the Role of Insurance:

Insurance is a risk management tool that protects individuals and families from financial losses due to unexpected events or emergencies. By transferring the risk to an insurance company in exchange for premium payments, individuals can mitigate the financial impact of unforeseen events and secure their financial future.
Insurance serves as a safety net, providing financial protection against risks such as illness, disability, death, accidents, natural disasters, and property damage. It helps individuals and families cope with the financial consequences of these events and maintain their standard of living.
Health Insurance:

Health insurance is a crucial component of financial planning, providing coverage for medical expenses and healthcare services. With the rising cost of healthcare, having adequate health insurance coverage is essential to protect against high medical bills and unexpected medical emergencies.

Health insurance can help individuals and families access timely medical care, prescription medications, hospitalization, and preventive services without incurring significant out-of-pocket expenses. It provides financial security and peace of mind knowing that you're protected against the financial burden of medical treatment.

Life Insurance:

Life insurance provides financial protection for your loved ones in the event of your death, helping to replace lost income, pay off debts, cover funeral expenses, and provide for your family's future financial needs. It serves as a financial safety net, ensuring that your family is taken care of financially if you're no longer there to provide for them.

There are different types of life insurance policies, including term life insurance, whole life insurance, and universal life insurance, each offering varying levels of coverage, premiums, and benefits. Choose a life insurance policy that aligns with your financial goals, budget, and family's needs.

Property Insurance:

Property insurance protects your physical assets, such as your home, car, or belongings, against loss or damage due to unforeseen events such as fire, theft, vandalism, or natural disasters. It provides financial compensation to repair or replace damaged property, helping you recover from unexpected losses and rebuild your life.

Homeowners insurance, renters insurance, and auto insurance are common types of property insurance that provide coverage for your home, personal property, and vehicles. Review your insurance policies regularly to ensure you have adequate coverage and are protected against potential risks.

Additional Types of Insurance:

Disability Insurance: Disability insurance provides income replacement if you're unable to work due to a disabling injury or illness. It helps you maintain your standard of living and meet your financial obligations during periods of disability when you're unable to earn an income.

Long-Term Care Insurance: Long-term care insurance provides coverage for the cost of long-term care services, such as nursing home care, assisted living, or home healthcare, in the event of a chronic illness, disability, or cognitive impairment. It helps protect your assets and preserve your financial independence in retirement.

Evaluating Insurance Needs:

Assess your insurance needs based on your financial situation, lifestyle, family circumstances, and risk tolerance. Consider factors such as your age, health status, income, assets, dependents, and financial goals when determining the appropriate types and amounts of insurance coverage.

Review your insurance policies regularly to ensure they're up to date, adequately cover your needs, and provide sufficient protection against potential risks. Update your coverage as needed to reflect changes in your life circumstances, such as marriage, childbirth, home purchase, or career advancement.

In conclusion, insurance plays a vital role in financial planning by providing protection against unforeseen events and helping individuals and families manage financial risks effectively. Health insurance, life insurance, property insurance, and other types of insurance serve as essential safeguards for your financial well-being, providing peace of mind and security in times of uncertainty. By evaluating your insurance needs, obtaining adequate coverage, and regularly reviewing your insurance policies, you can protect your finances and build a solid foundation for your future financial security.

Chapter: Estate Planning: Guidance on Wills, Trusts, and Preserving Your Legacy

Estate planning is a crucial aspect of financial planning that involves arranging for the distribution of your assets and the management of your affairs after your death or incapacitation. In this chapter, we'll explore the importance of estate planning and provide guidance on creating wills and trusts to preserve your legacy and protect your loved ones.

Understanding Estate Planning:

Estate planning is the process of making arrangements for the management and distribution of your assets and affairs upon your death or in the event of your incapacity. It involves creating legal documents and strategies to ensure your wishes are carried out and your loved ones are provided for according to your wishes.

Estate planning allows you to maintain control over your assets during your lifetime, minimize taxes, avoid probate, protect your beneficiaries, and preserve your legacy for future generations.

Creating a Will:

A will is a legal document that outlines your wishes regarding the distribution of your assets, guardianship of minor children, and the appointment of an executor to administer your estate. It allows you to specify who will inherit your property and how it will be divided among your beneficiaries. When creating a will, consider the following:

Identify your assets: Compile a list of your assets, including real estate, investments, bank accounts, retirement accounts, and personal belongings.

Choose beneficiaries: Decide who will inherit your assets and specify the percentage or share of the estate each beneficiary will receive.

Appoint an executor: Select a trustworthy individual to serve as the executor of your estate, responsible for carrying out the terms of your will and settling your affairs.

Plan for contingencies: Include provisions for unforeseen circumstances, such as the incapacity or death of a beneficiary or executor, to ensure your wishes are still fulfilled.

Review and update regularly: Regularly review and update your will to reflect changes in your family circumstances, assets, or wishes.

Understanding Trusts:

A trust is a legal arrangement in which one party (the grantor) transfers assets to another party (the trustee) to hold and manage for the benefit of designated beneficiaries. Trusts offer flexibility, control, and privacy in estate planning and can be used to achieve various objectives, such as asset protection, tax planning, and providing for minor children or individuals with special needs.

Common types of trusts include revocable living trusts, irrevocable trusts, testamentary trusts, and special needs trusts. Each type of trust has unique characteristics and purposes, so it's essential to choose the right trust structure based on your goals and circumstances.

Creating Trusts:

Determine your objectives: Clarify your goals and objectives for creating a trust, such as asset protection, avoiding probate, minimizing taxes, providing for minor children, or supporting charitable causes.

Select the appropriate trust structure: Choose the type of trust that aligns with your goals and circumstances, considering factors such as control, flexibility, taxation, and asset protection.

Identify beneficiaries and assets: Specify the beneficiaries who will benefit from the trust and the assets that will be transferred into the trust.

Appoint a trustee: Select a competent and trustworthy individual or institution to serve as the trustee responsible for managing the trust assets and carrying out the terms of the trust.

Draft the trust document: Work with an experienced estate planning attorney to draft the trust document, outlining the terms, conditions, and instructions governing the trust's administration and distribution of assets.

Fund the trust: Transfer ownership of assets into the trust by re-titling assets in the name of the trust or designating the trust as the beneficiary of accounts and policies.

Reviewing and Updating Estate Plans:

Estate planning is not a one-time event but an ongoing process that requires regular review and updating to reflect changes in your life circumstances, family dynamics, financial situation, and tax laws.

Review your estate plan periodically, especially after major life events such as marriage, divorce, childbirth, death of a beneficiary, acquisition or sale of assets, or changes in tax laws.

Update your will, trusts, and other estate planning documents as needed to ensure they accurately reflect your wishes and provide for the needs of your loved ones.

In conclusion, estate planning is essential for preserving your legacy, protecting your loved ones, and ensuring your assets are distributed according to your wishes. By creating wills and trusts, you can establish a comprehensive estate plan that provides peace of mind and safeguards your family's financial future. Consult with an experienced estate planning attorney to develop a customized estate plan tailored to your goals and circumstances, and review and update your plan regularly to adapt to changes in your life and the legal landscape. By taking initiative-taking steps to plan your estate, you can leave a legacy and provide for your loved ones for generations to come.

Chapter: Safeguarding Against Financial Fraud and Identity Theft

In this chapter, we'll explore essential tips for protecting yourself against financial fraud and identity theft, two prevalent threats that can have devastating consequences for your financial well-being and personal security. By implementing proactive measures and staying vigilant, you can minimize the risk of falling victim to fraudsters and safeguard your financial assets and personal information.

Stay Informed and Aware:

Educate yourself about common types of financial fraud and identity theft schemes, such as phishing scams, identity theft, credit card fraud, and investment scams. Stay informed about emerging threats and fraud trends to recognize potential red flags and protect yourself effectively.
Monitor reputable sources of information, such as government agencies, consumer protection organizations, and financial institutions, for alerts and updates on current scams and fraud warnings.
Protect Your Personal Information:

Safeguard sensitive personal information, such as Social Security numbers, financial account numbers, passwords, and login credentials, from unauthorized access or disclosure. Avoid sharing personal information online or over the phone unless you're certain of the recipient's identity and legitimacy.

Use strong, unique passwords for online accounts and consider enabling multi-factor authentication for added security. Avoid using easily guessable passwords or sharing passwords across multiple accounts.
Be Skeptical and Vigilant:

Exercise caution when responding to unsolicited emails, phone calls, or messages requesting personal or financial information. Be skeptical of unexpected or urgent requests for sensitive information and verify the legitimacy of the sender or caller before providing any details.
Watch for warning signs of potential scams, such as requests for upfront payments, pressure to act quickly, promises of unrealistic returns or prizes, or requests for remote access to your computer or devices.
Secure Your Devices and Accounts:

Keep your computer, smartphone, and other devices secure by installing reputable antivirus software, firewalls, and security updates regularly. Enable automatic updates and use encryption and password protection to secure sensitive data stored on your devices.
Secure your financial accounts with strong authentication methods, such as biometric authentication, security questions, or one-time passcodes sent via text message or email. Monitor your accounts regularly for unauthorized transactions or suspicious activity.
Shred Sensitive Documents:

Dispose of paper documents containing sensitive personal or financial information securely by shredding them before discarding. This includes bank statements, credit card statements, tax documents, and any other paperwork containing sensitive details that could be used for identity theft.
Review Your Credit Report Regularly:

Request and review your credit report from each of the three major credit bureaus—Equifax, Experian, and TransUnion—at least once a year. Check for any inaccuracies, discrepancies, or unauthorized accounts that could indicate identity theft or fraudulent activity.

Consider enrolling in a credit monitoring service or identity theft protection service that provides ongoing monitoring of your credit report and alerts you to any suspicious changes or activity.

Report Suspected Fraud Immediately:

If you suspect you've fallen victim to financial fraud or identity theft, act quickly to minimize the damage and protect yourself. Contact your financial institutions, credit card issuers, and relevant authorities, such as the Federal Trade Commission (FTC) or local law enforcement, to report the incident and initiate fraud resolution procedures.

Place a fraud alert or credit freeze on your credit report to prevent further unauthorized activity and notify the major credit bureaus of the potential fraud.

By following these tips and remaining vigilant, you can reduce the risk of falling victim to financial fraud and identity theft and protect yourself against potential financial losses and personal harm. Remember that prevention is key, so take proactive steps to safeguard your personal information, stay informed about emerging threats, and trust your instincts if something seems suspicious. With diligence and awareness, you can protect your financial assets and preserve your peace of mind in an increasingly digital and interconnected world.

Conclusion: Safeguarding Your Financial Future

In "Saving Money Book," we've covered a comprehensive range of topics aimed at empowering readers to take control of their finances, achieve their financial goals, and build a secure future. Here are the key points summarized from the book:

Understanding Financial Basics:

We explored the fundamentals of personal finance, budgeting, and money management, providing readers with the foundational knowledge needed to make informed financial decisions.
Setting Financial Goals:

We emphasized the importance of setting clear, achievable financial goals and provided guidance on creating SMART goals tailored to individual needs and aspirations.
Budgeting and Money Management:

Readers learned practical strategies for creating and maintaining a budget, tracking expenses, and adjusting spending habits to align with their financial goals and priorities.
Saving and Investing Wisely:

We discussed various strategies for saving money, including cutting expenses, negotiating bills, automating savings, and building emergency funds. Additionally, readers gained insights into investment fundamentals, diversification, and risk management to grow their wealth effectively.

Managing Debt:

We addressed the challenges of debt management and offered strategies for paying off debt efficiently, avoiding high-interest debt, and using credit responsibly to maintain financial health.

Maximizing Income:

Readers explored opportunities for increasing income through side hustles, freelancing, career advancement, and negotiation techniques, empowering them to enhance their earning potential and financial security.

Protecting Your Finances:

We highlighted the importance of insurance in financial planning, including health, life, property, and other types of insurance, to mitigate risks and safeguard against unexpected events.

Estate Planning:

We provided guidance on estate planning, wills, and trusts, enabling readers to protect their assets, preserve their legacy, and ensure their loved ones are provided for according to their wishes.

Safeguarding Against Financial Fraud and Identity Theft:

Finally, we offered tips for protecting against financial fraud and identity theft, empowering readers to stay informed, secure their personal information, and recognize and respond to potential scams effectively.

By incorporating these key principles and strategies into their financial planning, readers can build a solid foundation for financial stability, security, and prosperity. "Saving Money Book" equips readers with the knowledge, tools, and confidence they need to navigate the complexities of personal finance and achieve their long-term financial goals. With diligence, discipline, and ongoing education, readers can embark on a journey towards financial empowerment and a brighter financial future.

Chapter: Take Action: Transforming Knowledge into Financial Success

Now that you've gained valuable insights and strategies from "Saving Money Book," it's time to turn that knowledge into action and embark on your journey toward financial success. In this chapter, I'll encourage you to take proactive steps to implement the strategies outlined in the book and start transforming your financial future.

Commit to Change:

The first step toward financial success is making a commitment to change. Take ownership of your financial situation and recognize that you have the power to shape your financial future. Embrace a positive mindset and believe in your ability to achieve your goals.
Set Clear Goals:

Take the time to define your financial goals with clarity and specificity. Whether it's building an emergency fund, paying off debt, saving for a home, or planning for retirement, clearly defined goals provide direction and motivation for action.
Create a Plan:

Develop a comprehensive financial plan that outlines the steps you need to take to achieve your goals. Break down your goals into smaller, manageable tasks and prioritize them based on urgency and importance. A well-crafted plan serves as your roadmap to success.

Take Small Steps:

Don't feel overwhelmed by the magnitude of your financial goals. Start by taking small, achievable steps toward progress. Whether it's tracking your expenses, negotiating bills, or setting up automatic savings, every action you take brings you closer to your goals.

Track Your Progress:

Monitor your progress regularly and celebrate your achievements along the way. Use tools like budgeting apps, spreadsheets, or financial tracking software to keep tabs on your income, expenses, savings, and investment growth. Tracking your progress helps you stay motivated and accountable.

Stay Disciplined and Consistent:

Building financial success requires discipline and consistency. Stay committed to your financial plan, even when faced with challenges or setbacks. Make wise financial choices and resist the temptation to deviate from your plan in favor of short-term gratification.

Educate Yourself Continuously:

Continue to educate yourself about personal finance and seek opportunities for learning and growth. Stay informed about financial trends, investment opportunities, and strategies for wealth-building. Knowledge is power, and ongoing education empowers you to make informed decisions.

Seek Support and Accountability:

Surround yourself with a supportive network of friends, family, or financial advisors who can offer guidance, encouragement, and accountability. Share your goals and progress with trusted individuals who can provide feedback, advice, and moral support along the way.

Adapt and Adjust:

Be flexible and adaptable in your approach to financial planning. Life circumstances and financial markets are constantly changing, so be prepared to adjust your plan as needed. Embrace change as an opportunity for growth and learning, and remain open to new possibilities.

Celebrate Your Successes:

Finally, don't forget to celebrate your successes and milestones along your financial journey. Whether it's reaching a savings goal, paying off a debt, or achieving a milestone in your investment portfolio, take the time to acknowledge and reward yourself for your hard work and perseverance.

By taking action and implementing the strategies outlined in "Saving Money Book," you can transform your financial future and achieve the financial success you desire. Remember that every step you take brings you closer to your goals, so don't hesitate to start today. With determination, discipline, and a commitment to lifelong learning, you can build a brighter financial future for yourself and your loved ones.

Chapter: Believe in Your Financial Potential: Achieving Stability and Success Through Saving Money

As you journey through the pages of "Saving Money Book," I want to instill within you a profound sense of confidence in your ability to achieve financial stability and success through the power of saving money. In this chapter, I'll express unwavering belief in your financial potential and highlight the transformative impact that saving money can have on your life.

You Have the Power to Change Your Financial Future:

No matter your current financial situation, I want you to know that you possess the power to change your financial future for the better. By embracing the principles of saving money outlined in this book and taking proactive steps to implement them in your life, you can chart a new course toward financial stability and success.
Small Actions Lead to Significant Results:

It's important to recognize that even the smallest actions can lead to significant results when it comes to saving money. Whether it's cutting unnecessary expenses, automating your savings, or negotiating bills, each step you take brings you closer to your financial goals and builds momentum for future success.
Believe in the Power of Consistency:

Consistency is key when it comes to saving money. By making saving a consistent habit in your daily life, you'll gradually build a strong financial foundation and create opportunities for long-term growth and prosperity. Trust in the power of consistency to propel you toward your financial goals.

Celebrate Your Progress Along the Way:

As you embark on your journey toward financial stability and success, don't forget to celebrate your progress along the way. Whether it's reaching a savings milestone, paying off a debt, or achieving a financial goal, take the time to acknowledge and celebrate your achievements. Each success is a testament to your dedication and determination.

You Are Capable of Overcoming Challenges:

It's natural to encounter challenges and obstacles on your path to financial success. However, I want you to know that you are capable of overcoming these challenges with resilience, perseverance, and a positive attitude. Believe in your ability to navigate through financial challenges and emerge stronger on the other side.

Embrace a Growth Mindset:

Adopting a growth mindset is essential for achieving financial stability and success. Instead of viewing setbacks as failures, see them as opportunities for growth and learning. Embrace challenges as stepping stones toward your goals and remain open to new possibilities and opportunities for improvement.

Visualize Your Financial Success:

Take a moment to visualize your financial success and the life you desire to create for yourself and your loved ones. Picture yourself achieving your goals, enjoying financial freedom, and living a life of abundance and fulfillment. Use this vision as motivation to stay focused and committed to your financial journey.

Believe in Yourself and Your Potential:

Above all, believe in yourself and your potential to achieve financial stability and success through saving money. You possess the skills, knowledge, and determination needed to create the life you envision for yourself. Trust in your abilities and have faith in the process of saving money to lead you toward your desired financial future.

As you continue your journey through "Saving Money Book," I encourage you to hold onto this sense of confidence and belief in your financial potential. With dedication, perseverance, and a commitment to saving money, you can overcome obstacles, achieve your goals, and create the financial future you deserve. Remember, the power to transform your financial life lies within you.

www.ingramcontent.com/pod-product-compliance
Lightning Source LLC
Chambersburg PA
CBHW050329230526
45471CB00005B/2410